ADJUSTMENTS

AFFIRMATIONS FOR INNER ECOLOGY

by Sônia Café
Illustrations by Neide Innecco

SAMUEL WEISER, INC.
York Beach, Maine

First published in 1999 by
Samuel Weiser, Inc.
P. O. Box 612
York Beach, ME 03910-0612
www.weiserbooks.com

Copyright © 1999 Sônia Café and Neide Innecco
All rights reserved.
No part of this publication may be reproduced or transmitted
in any form or by any means, electronic or mechanical, including
photocopying, recording, or by any information storage and retrieval
system, without permission in writing from Samuel Weiser, Inc.
Reviewers may quote brief passages. First published as *O Livro das
Atitudes* by Editora Pensamento, Brazil, copyright © 1992 Editora
Pensamento, Ltda.

Café, Sônia.
  [Livro das atitudes. English]
  Attitude adjustments : affirmations for inner ecology /
Sônia Café : illustrated by Neide Innecco.
    p.   cm.
  Includes index.
  ISBN 1-57863-025-8 (paper : alk. paper)
  1. Attitude (Psychology). 2. Affirmations. I. Title
BL927.C3413 1999
153.8`5--dc21   98-53593
                                                          CIP

Typeset in 10 point Bembo
Printed and bound in Hong Kong
08 07 06 05 04 03 02 01 00 99
  10 9 8 7 6 5 4 3 2 1
C&C

The paper used in this publication meets all the minimum
requirements of the American National Standard for Permanence of
Paper for Printed Library Materials Z39.48–1984.

Contents

Introduction 1
How to Use this Set 4
Develop a Bold Attitude 8
Develop an Efficient Attitude 10
Develop a Decisive Attitude 12
Develop a Cooperative Attitude 14
Develop a Loving Attitude 16
Develop a Generous Attitude 18
Develop a Wise Attitude 20
Develop an Alternative Attitude 22
Develop an Adaptable Attitude 24
Develop a Diplomatic Attitude 26
Develop a Participatory Attitude 28
Develop a Truthful Attitude 30
Develop a Responsible Attitude 32
Develop an Appreciative Attitude 34
Develop a Pure Attitude 36
Develop a Sensual Attitude 38
Develop a Joyful Attitude 40
Develop a Consistent Attitude 42
Develop an Impeccable Attitude 44
Develop a Pleasurable Attitude 46

Develop a Focused Attitude	48
Develop a Meditative Attitude	50
Develop a Persevering Attitude	52
Develop a Reverent Attitude	54
Develop a Mature Attitude	56
Develop an Altruistic Attitude	58
Develop a Giving Attitude	60
Develop a Liberating Attitude	62
Develop a Paternal Attitude	64
Develop a Compassionate Attitude	66
Develop a Pragmatic Attitude	68
Develop a Poetic Attitude	70
Develop a Modest Attitude	72
Develop an Innocent Attitude	74
Develop a Telepathic Attitude	76
Develop a Harmonious Attitude	78
Develop an Intuitive Attitude	80
Develop an Enthusiastic Attitude	82
Develop an Organized Attitude	84
Develop a Tolerant Attitude	86
Develop a Tranquil Attitude	88
Develop a Sensitive Attitude	90
Develop a Passionate Attitude	92
Develop a Rational Attitude	94
Develop a Patient Attitude	96

Develop a Synergistic Attitude 98
Develop a Flexible Attitude 100
Develop a Thankful Attitude 102
Develop a Receptive Attitude 104
Develop a Positive Attitude. 106
Develop a Transformative Attitude 108
Develop an Optimistic Attitude. 110
Develop a Maternal Attitude. 112
Develop a Healing Attitude. 114
Develop a Committed Attitude 116
Develop a Supportive Attitude 118
Develop a Practical Attitude 120
Develop a Sincere Attitude 122
Develop a Harmless Attitude. 124
Develop a Connected Attitude 126
Develop an Intelligent Attitude 128
Develop a Detached Attitude 130
Develop a Dynamic Attitude. 132
Develop a Healthy Attitude. 134
Index. 136
About the Author 137
About the Illustrator 138

Introduction

We can always develop and manifest attitudes through thoughts, feelings, body gestures, and words. Every attitude asks for a form of action that can be visible or invisible to the eye. This action will lead us into a process in which we will be invoking the essential qualities that we want to see manifested in our lives. Whenever we understand something intellectually, we create a need to anchor that understanding within the heart, for then any action that comes from that blend will be inspiring for everyone concerned.

There are an infinite number of ways to take action, and every action implies a choice that is immediately reflected in the environment where we live. When we are aware of the way we act, our actions will be enriched by the kind of attitude we choose to assume, and we create a luminous and synchronistic web of quality that allows everything to flow in tune with our choices. We know what we are choosing and how our choices are affecting the whole.

So, conscious and lovingly assumed attitudes are the key to leading a life in tune with our true Essence. Responding—here and now—to what life brings, with the best or most appropriate gesture, feeling, or thought is the greatest gift we can give and receive as human beings.

All kinds of visible and invisible beings are deeply and energetically interacting in nature; we live in a multidimensional reality. The universe is ever-changing. In the middle of all this wonder of life, we human beings play a very important part in creating and sharing consciousness with life on many levels. The quality of how human life changes through evolution depends a lot on the attitudes we decide to nourish and develop as a species.

When a flower blooms in a forest and a hummingbird comes to drink its nectar, one feels the presence of joy in the vulnerability of the flower that opens itself and surrenders to the kiss of the bird. In Nature, "attitudes" are organically inspired and reflect a precious gift of synchronicity and interdependence that connects everything in a web of life and meaning.

Human beings are the only group in that web that can consciously choose the direction of their actions and make visible the intentions of their Divine Essence and, through their attitudes, demonstrate the value of their words, the power of their thoughts, and the warmth of their feelings in everything they do.

When we perform any action, be it simply thinking, feeling, or taking into account the fact that non-action at the right time is also a form of action, conscious of the best attitude for each moment, we create an openness to the deeper dimensions of our Self, where we have access to limitless love and wisdom.

The quality present in our consciousness when we develop or assume attitudes is what determines the vibratory field where we will act and live out our knowledge of being simultaneously human and divine.

How to Use this Set

This book and deck invite you to become aware of the importance of your attitudes, and how they reflect what you attract and create in the day-to-day of your life.

If you are conscious of the attitude you assume during certain situations, you will be using your creative potential to its fullest, responding with love and intelligence to the challenges that life may bring.

Attitude Adjustments: Affirmations for Inner Ecology intends to be a conscious link between you and the environment where you live. Use it when you need a friend to help you in the search for an attitude that will best suit your plan of action. Take into account the following points:

- It is the conscious attunement that you create with your own Soul or Inner Essence that attracts and manifests acts of synchronicity in your life. It is your Soul that will inspire you to get in touch with the right page of this book. Or you may decide to pick a card from the deck at random, and work on that particular quality for a day or a week.

- Make a moment of silence to create a conscious connection with your Inner Essence so you can see the greater whole of the issue you want to approach.

- Visualize, or write, or speak aloud the question or the situation on which you want to focus—where you would like to have some guidance. Open your mind's heart to receive it.

- As you use this book you will find reflexive text on the left-hand page. The illustration may inspire you with meaningful images or associations for you at that moment. On the right you will find suggestions to help you practice that attitude in your life. The cards offer an affirmation to use to help you develop each attitude.

Attitude Adjustments: Affirmations for Inner Ecology can also be used to inspire conscious attitudes in people who work together in a group, or who share the same purpose and are willing to grow and evolve together.

You will find that a variety of Nature beings illustrate attitudes that we can assume. At the same time, you are being invited to become aware of the many levels of life and intelligence that inhabit the different dimensions of our beautiful planet Earth.

May you have wonderful moments of Soul connection and may your conscious attitudes transform and heal your life!

*This book is dedicated,
With loving gratitude
To the Angel of Nazaré
Who touched me deep in the Soul?
And opened doors of perception.*

*"The greatest revolution of our times is the
discovery that by changing the inner attitudes of our
minds we can change the outer
aspects of our lives."*

(LIGHTLY ADAPTED FROM A FAMOUS QUOTE BY
WILLIAM JAMES)

Develop a Bold Attitude

*R*eason doesn't always know the right way to action. There are moments when you will only know how to act after having taken the first step toward the unknown. When you perceive that your Soul, from somewhere with broader vision, can see the map of the whole territory of your life, you can release your need to intellectualize and be in control all the time. The spirit of the pioneer knows the real value of developing a daring attitude. You can be bold, daring, adventuresome, and try something new.

Practical Suggestions for a Bold Attitude

- Do something that may feel "daring" to you. This does not mean that you should put yourself or others in danger.

- Fear not walking toward the unknown.

- Ask someone to be tender with you, or ask for anything that you would not normally dare to ask for. (Take the risk of having no attachment to the results of your action.)

- Take the first step to reestablish a positive and loving communication in a relationship.

- Risk laughing or crying whenever it feels right to you.

Develop an Efficient Attitude

*T*he time has come to get the needed results. Efficiency is always present when you are ready to follow the greater purpose of your life. When the direction is clear, action becomes ordered and decisive, leading to the accomplishment of the task facing you. The results are always the best. When you really love what you do, you are going to be efficient.

Practical Suggestions for an Efficient Attitude

- See if your goals are clear.
- Have you defined the priorities in your life?
- Finish that task you have started for it is waiting for a conclusion.
- Get your life updated (correspondence, bills, phone calls, etc.).

Develop a Decisive Attitude

When you develop a decisive attitude, you release the passive condition of "wishful thinking" and get right into action! Wishing can lead to inertia and separates you from what you really want to create. A clear and healthy will is necessary so you can choose one alternative, leaving aside, momentarily, all other options. In this way, you allow the life energy to flow again. Experimenting consciously and willfully gives expression to the capacity of self-determination that you carry in your Soul. Maybe this is a moment to leave passivity aside and make a very important decision.

Practical Suggestions for a Decisive Attitude

- Willingness to change is a powerful issue. Are you willing to stop a habit that is doing you no good?

- Use your willpower to make positive and constructive affirmations in your life.

- Be proactive—negative and automatic reactions drain your vitality away.

- Find a treat that your "inner child" loves and give it to her.

Develop a Cooperative Attitude

Where there is cooperation there are no power struggles. The cooperative attitude is the one that emphasizes the converging points within a group or in a relationship, to create empathy and partnership. When you cooperate, recognizing the dignity in every human being, and the contribution each can make, your personal power is transformed into service for the good of all beings in your environment. The works of Nature are the most beautiful lessons of what cooperation really means.

Practical Suggestions for a Cooperative Attitude

- See if there is someone, here and now, who needs your cooperation.

- Be mindful regarding the clarity and full understanding of the common goals in any undertaking or task.

- To be cooperative it is important to know how to listen. Recognize the ideas and visions of other people within a group or in a relationship.

- Cooperate with the global quality of life: support the recycling of natural resources.

Develop a Loving Attitude

Love is the essential motivation in all we do. Your motivation can be an intense and burning desire to love and be loved, a conscious expression of fraternal and friendly love, or an encompassing and unconditional love that you allow to flow through you for everyone and everything. A loving attitude is healing and it transforms any blocks in the way to self-realization.

Practical Suggestions for a Loving Attitude

- Love can be expressed in infinite ways. Discover your unique and incomparable way of loving and love a lot.

- Open your heart to simple acts of service to people, to animals, to plants, to the whole of Nature.

- Transform your demands into preferences. To "prefer" that something be a certain way is more liberating and loving than to "demand" something be the way you think it should be.

- Never forget that love starts with you. First you discover it within. This is a key to feel that love is flowing in all directions and fulfilling your life.

Develop a Generous Attitude

*E*verything in Nature is spontaneously generous. You can act, feel, and think generously. When you act generously, you start from a consciousness of prosperity and abundance, and the emphasis is on the quality—not on the quantity—of whatever you do. When you feel generous, the act of giving is spontaneous and invisible. When you think generously, you understand that the joy of giving and the full capacity of receiving are parts of the same, unique gift.

Practical Suggestions for a Generous Attitude

- See if there is something that you can give someone that will make him or her very happy.

- Become aware of what you have generously received from someone and give thanks from your heart.

- Receive with joy the blessings of life, reflected in a sunny day, in the singing of a bird, in the air you breathe, in the one driving the bus that takes you home . . .

- Never tire of giving thanks. Gratitude is the nourishment that feeds the generosity within.

- Practice the act of giving with no expectation of receiving in return. This will lead you to discover how the Law of Abundance works.

Develop a Wise Attitude

To act with wisdom you need to open your heart and invoke the presence of the Divine Consciousness within. The wise attitude emerges gradually, when you recognize the need to learn with every experience that is to be lived with wholeness, no matter if it is positive or negative. The Wisdom that comes from the Soul teaches you to see beyond appearances and to go directly to the real meaning of each happening in God's magnificent Universe.

Practical Suggestions for a Wise Attitude

- See if you have been listening to your inner voice and obeying the Soul's directions.

- Look at the reality of things without denial or pre-judgment.

- Accept the way things are without antagonisms, feel the energy that comes to accomplish everything that needs to be done.

- There is a time for everything. Give time to time.

Develop an Alternative Attitude

When you keep yourself attached to habit patterns or conditioning, or when you allow yourself to be limited by beliefs that belong to the past, the time has come to develop an alternative attitude. This attitude allows a search for new perspectives and possibilities that you hadn't been aware of before. If you do this, you exercise freely the power of choice without the imposition of limiting beliefs because you perceive the variety and diversity available to you.

Practical Suggestions for an Alternative Attitude

- Feel free to choose. Do not allow an excess of traditionalism hinder your way to see new and promising horizons.

- Give support to the appearance of new experience in your life.

- Choose, more and more, to support the balance between what you need and the nonrenewable resources of Nature.

- Try to identify all the things that can make your life easier and more coherent with what you really think, feel, and do. For example, get rid of the clutter that complicates your life.

Develop an Adaptable Attitude

You need to be very adaptable because of the fast pace of our world today. In your Soul you have a great capacity to be adaptable, because on that level of consciousness and being you are very much aware of the impermanence of things. You find true adaptability when you choose to contact your Divine Essence, for then you can stop resisting those inevitable changes that life will bring. If you are steady in the search for self-knowledge, you will recognize the need for an adaptable attitude.

Practical Suggestions for an Adaptable Attitude

- Relax in relation to the time on the clock. Try to discover an "inner time," which is less chronological, and experiment with being always "on the right time."

- If you lead a sedentary kind of life, start doing something to stimulate and bring vitality to your body.

- Look at all your relationships as processes of learning and growth that lead you to know yourself better.

- Be aware of inertia. Adaptability is not conformity.

Develop a Diplomatic Attitude

It is possible that you need to act diplomatically in a delicate or critical situation. Gentleness and tact will help you avoid clashes and misunderstandings. The precise and kind gesture, the correct word, can alleviate stressful situations in your environment as well as within your own consciousness.

Practical Suggestions for a Diplomatic Attitude

- Affirm your own value, but do not demand recognition.

- Refuse elegantly to accept anything that may humiliate or depreciate yourself and others.

- Take care that negative or overly-emotionalized thoughts do not interfere with the connection between yourself and your Inner Divinity.

- Speak clearly and rhythmically, becoming aware of the value and power of your words.

Develop a Participatory Attitude

When the light of the Soul begins to radiate through your life, you feel a great impulse to participate in the healing and transformation of the planet. This is so because you know that you can never be isolated or separated from your human brothers and sisters, or from the whole of Nature. When you develop a participatory attitude, you are being stimulated to share with the "greater whole" the meaning of your singularity and uniqueness. You are also adding value to the quality of consciousness being generated in the community where you live.

Practical Suggestions for a Participatory Attitude

- Share with the people that you love all that you have learned and discovered about yourself lately.

- Recognize the changes in your life that have led you to be more participating and alive.

- You are a special and unique person in the universe. Know that and participate in life with joy.

- In group activities, in a couple relationship, in family gatherings, participate with attentive listening, with clear vision, and loving-kindness to all including yourself.

Develop a Truthful Attitude

*T*he originality of every child lies in the wonderful capacity of genuine self-expression. The "eternal child" that lives within you will easily invite you to seek truth in any situation. You can surprise yourself with your own spontaneity and fearlessness when you reveal your true face. When you are genuine, you are free of the mask that may veil the expression of your true identity.

Practical Suggestions for a Truthful Attitude

- What is the truest answer you will give yourself today when asked: "Who are you?"

- Do what you said you would do.

- When you make a mistake, admit it. But don't feel guilty. Guilt will encourage you to feel you have the right to make the same mistake again.

- Welcome your "inner child," for this part of you knows, more than anyone else, how to laugh, how to have fun, and, most of all, how to be true to yourself.

Develop a Responsible Attitude

You change the world by changing yourself. To do that you need to be responsible. The responsible attitude strengthens your character, if you respond to what is asked of you from a center of inner joy and trust. This inner center, your Soul, transmutes the weight of duty and obligation into lightness and ability to respond to what life is proposing. To act responsibly is to give yourself the joyful pleasure of putting into practice your best talents and skill.

Practical Suggestions for a Responsible Attitude

- Assume total responsibility for your own well-being. You are a very talented person.

- Feel that you deserve magnificent gifts from God.

- Make a list of the talents and abilities that you have. Recognize the things that you love doing and do things with love. Feel how light is the weight of responsibility.

- See the direction you want to follow in your life. As you are a responsible person, all your experiences will be transformed into a very rich learning process.

Develop an Appreciative Attitude

Consciousness expands and vibrates in every sentient being when you look at them with eyes that know how to appreciate. The value of appreciation lies in knowing that everyone is subtly connected, and the lightest wave of appreciation is enough to lift your spirits and change any challenging situation. Appreciative behavior is the genuine expression of your capacity to generate positive energy continually, recognizing the real essence and contributions that come from the people and situations around you.

Practical Suggestions for an Appreciative Attitude

- Practice appreciation by affirming the positive and creative points in people and situations of life.

- Hug at least four people today. Tell them what you appreciate in them.

- Recognize and affirm what you most appreciate in yourself.

- Surprise someone by sending a note of appreciation. For example: "Dear . . . Thank you for being so caring and for having such a good sense of humor." Or, "I deeply appreciate your growing capacity to love."

Develop a Pure Attitude

*E*very action that is performed with a feeling of wholeness in the heart is organically and essentially pure. To develop a pure attitude it is necessary to choose to go beyond conflict, fear, and illusion. When you do that, you are saying yes to a process of inner purification in the "environment" of your consciousness. You are essentially pure whenever your thoughts, emotions, and actions are in tune with the greater vision of your Soul.

Practical Suggestions for a Pure Attitude

- Start your day as if you were facing everything for the first time. Allow yourself to be renewed and feel a rebirth is being inspired by your conscious contacts with a living Nature.

- Negative thoughts pollute the body and the environment very quickly. Watch the flow of your thinking.

- Do anything that makes you feel pure. For example, drink a lot of pure water; take a special bath; listen to good music; have some quiet time and in the silence surrender yourself to your Soul; say a prayer . . .

- Visualize your whole being in the most sublime light of the Soul, and feel the powerful purifying energies that emanate from this experience.

Develop a Sensual Attitude

The sensual attitude is the one that makes you truly aware of your senses. It invites you to be present with your whole being—whenever you touch, listen, or look intentionally at someone or something, when you taste nourishing food, or smell fragrances. When developing a sensual attitude, you are led to experiment with the principle of unity, which lies behind everything that is lived consciously and lovingly with your senses. When you are sensually aware, your Divine Essence is filled with gratification, and you are free from the illusion of separateness.

Practical Suggestions for a Sensual Attitude

- Don't be afraid of feeling pleasure. Pleasure is more intense when you feel it with the Soul.

- Meditate on the following: experiences with your senses (vision, hearing, smell, taste, and touch) are direct, nontransferable, and essentially unifying.

- Be aware of what you can discover with your senses. When the five senses are fulfilled, there are many more subtle ones to be discovered and developed.

- Delight yourself in the wonderful senses the Creator has given you. The greatest sin is to dull or blunt those divine gifts.

Develop a Joyful Attitude

Joy and lightness are inseparable companions. You cannot assume a joyful attitude in life while you feel the heaviness of judgment, envy, suspicion, jealousy, or any other negative forms of thinking and feeling. Joy invites laughter, and laughter is good for the heart and for the digestive system. It also strengthens the muscles and activates the creative functions in the brain. When you choose the way of joy, all your attitudes are enhanced with a special brightness, brilliance, and splendor.

Practical Suggestions for a Joyful Attitude

- Play more with the situations in your life. Don't take life so seriously.

- Sing more, dance more—even when your singing is silent or your dance is just walking through life.

- When was the last time you had a good laugh? If you don't remember, it's because it has been too long.

- What is more important to you? To be happy or to always be right?

Develop a Consistent Attitude

*T*o stay firm and decisive in a challenging situation is the true exercise of coherence or consistency. Your clarity of thought, the peacefulness of your emotions, and the evenness of your physical reactions need to be a reflex of your connection with the clear and consistent light of the Soul. Like a laser beam, you direct your focus firmly toward your goals and values, as you remember your unity with the whole of life.

Practical Suggestions for a Consistent Attitude

- If you are not living according to your vision, see if any past or present conflicts need your attention, so you can move forward.

- Walk your talk. Practice what you preach and see if you are consistent regarding your thinking, feeling, and the action you take.

- Meditate upon two apparently contradictory situations in your life. Raise your consciousness to a level of transcendence, beyond contradictions, and find a coherent meaning for them.

- Empower the words you say by avoiding idle conversation.

Develop an Impeccable Attitude

It is not uncommon to feel guilty about negative experiences from the past that you created because of a lack of perception. You may feel sorry for not having the loving-kindness and care that would make the difference. When you are willing to forgive yourself, the Soul gives you the gift of being able to free yourself of fault or blame—and even sin. An impeccable attitude will invite you to act according to the highest perception that you may have of others and yourself—one that goes beyond appearances and ego limitations. The eternal present is the only time and place where you can feel free of guilt and move ahead in the face of any situation.

Practical Suggestions for an Impeccable Attitude

- See if there are repetitive and negative patterns in your life. Recognize them as if they were prayer requests and liberate them in the light of the Soul.

- Forgive yourself for all experiences lived through in ignorance and in lack of love. Open your heart and allow your Divine Essence to fill it with forgiveness.

- Note three good qualities in someone with whom you may have no affinity.

- See how you can be of help to others without becoming a victim or a martyr. Surrender to God all your actions.

Develop a Pleasurable Attitude

The more you learn to love and approve of your Being with conscious self-acceptance, the more pleasurable your attitude will become. Pleasure becomes part of life when you are free from the need to please others just to have approval, or when you do the work necessary to establish your own self-esteem. Pleasure is attached to every action when you are able to recognize that love—for yourself and for others—is always there to share.

Practical Suggestions for a Pleasurable Attitude

- Do today whatever you most enjoy doing.

- Never put off until tomorrow what you can do, feel, and live today—with a lot of pleasure.

- When you do things, pay careful attention and discover how pleasurable they are.

- Love whatever you are doing. Feel the pleasure and make sure you are conscious of it. Some people save their pleasure for later—for what they think they will like doing better. Pleasure happens now.

Develop a Focused Attitude

When mental distractions begin to deviate your attention away from a constructive path, it's time to stop and concentrate your attention. The time has come to see what is truly relevant for the present moment. Your higher mind—the one that is clear, luminous, and creative—is always ready to serve you. Energy follows thought and your conscious awareness is what is going to determine the way you create your life at each moment. A focused attitude in face of certain challenges will intensify your energy so you can avoid unnecessary delays or problems.

Practical Suggestions for a Focused Attitude

- Do concentration exercises. At least once a week try to do something where you pay attention to every single detail. For example, weed the garden, water the plants, clean your house, wash dishes, etc.

- Slow down the speed with which you normally do things. If you always do a particular task in a hurry, slow down 50 percent. If you tend to be too slow or lazy, do the opposite—speed up 50 percent.

- Dedicate at least 15 minutes a day to listen carefully to what people around you say; listen to them with your full attention.

- In regular intervals during the day, remind yourself of the ones you love. Try to feel them close to your heart and imagine how that one person may be feeling. Send your loved one "concentrated" vibrations of love.

Develop a
Meditative Attitude

*T*o experiment with a meditative attitude it is necessary to understand the meaning of silence. And to do that, you need to recognize the value and power of word and sound. This is just the beginning; but when you stop the inner rattle and noise of past beliefs, conditionings, and ideologies, and surrender to inner silence, then you can see the real face of the Soul. And when you experience the "unity of life" in the center of your Being, everything becomes meditation.

Practical Suggestions for a Meditative Attitude

- Try to speak only when you are inspired to do it. Your voice will strengthen and your words will be transformed in pure vibration.

- Have some moments of quiet every day.

- See the real value in silence. Care for the tone of your voice and the volume of the sound equipment at home.

- Practice being in the presence of your Soul. Tune your heart with the present moment.

- Walk silently in Nature or in your city park. Be attuned to the natural sounds surrounding you.

Develop a Persevering Attitude

*P*erseverance always brings good results. Don't let contradictory influences of opposites discourage you. Your Soul will come to meet you and will help you transcend limitations. When you persist with rhythm and grace, and in tune with the signs that life brings, you are simultaneously purifying and transforming the "lead" of impatience and despondency into the "gold" of self-realization.

Practical Suggestions for a Persevering Attitude

- Bless the ones who may eventually bring challenges to your path. Notice how they bring important instructions and mirror facets of yourself of which you may not be aware.

- Bring the experiences you have learned from lately to your awareness.

- Do not give up when the first challenge arrives. Calm down. Breathe. Go forward.

- Be faithful to your highest ideals and beliefs. A truly conscious person is priceless.

Develop a
Reverent Attitude

*T*he reverent attitude can be expressed through tender feelings and a willingness to go deeper into your relationships with people and with all beings of Nature. A powerful storm, the gentle beauty of a flower, the mysterious process of the development of a baby in the womb—all inspire reverence for life. Your Soul will lead you into situations where you are invited to express a reverent devotion, and perceive the vast interconnection that exists among all beings. It is easy to be reverent when you delight and wonder in awe of the many miracles of life, and when you perceive the presence of the sacred in the most ordinary activity.

Practical Suggestions for a Reverent Attitude

- Go to a church or temple, or any sacred place, and—in silence—feel the presence of God, reverently.

- Give your parents a call (or think of them wherever they are) and tell them how much they're loved.

- Do something for the elderly or for the very young. Act, feel, and think of something that you can do to bring joy.

- Who have been the most important teachers in your life? Give yourself some time to remember and thank them for the instruction you have received.

- What have you been doing lately to add value to your life and to the environment where you live?

Develop a Mature Attitude

What are the talents and abilities you have naturally developed in your life? Recognize and affirm positively the value of your capacities, for this is a good way to stimulate the manifestation of a mature attitude. Maturity flows naturally when you are willing to recognize the processes of growth you've experienced. When you use your resources in situations where everyone will benefit, you are handling your life in a mature manner.

Practical Suggestions for a Mature Attitude

- Be 100 percent responsible for your life, and understand that you are the only one who can decide which way is the best one to follow now.

- Is there a young person who needs your care? Demonstrate your maturity to this child by offering love and security.

- Do not forget your inner child. A mature ego is open to the guidance that comes from the Soul and is ready to rescue the inner child when it is in trouble.

- Which are the mature fruits of your life? Which ones aren't ripe yet? The mature ones are ready to support you while you wait for the rest to ripen.

Develop an Altruistic Attitude

When you reach the higher and more loving levels of consciousness, you feel a deep joy in sharing your energy and vitality with others. When respond to the needs of others as if they were yours, you create a sense of oneness and abundance—naturally and in synchronicity. The altruistic attitude happens in a spontaneous and silent way, and aims for the good of others, be it a person or any creature in Nature. In this process, you learn that the more you give, the more you allow the flow of abundant and eternal life to be present in each act of selfless service.

Practical Suggestions for an Altruistic Attitude

- The path of service is a round one. The more you serve, the more you will be served. Practice acts of service spontaneously and selflessly.

- Nature desperately needs your altruism. Use all natural resources (air, food, fuels, paper, etc.) with a conscience and a lot of gratitude.

- Answer the needs of others as if they were yours. This puts into action a subtle law of abundance and prosperity.

- Within your home, see who's in need of your loving care and tenderness now.

Develop a Giving Attitude

Mother Earth provides for all creatures that live in her space without asking anything in return. When we human beings use all her resources correctly, we all receive everything we need. A "giving" attitude will open your mind to be able to see available resources. When you can give without asking anything in return, you will discover ways to nourish the people of the world with material, emotional, and mental resources, and can provide the means for everything to happen effectively.

Practical Suggestions for a Giving Attitude

- See if there is any "stagnant energy" in your home or in your work environment. Allow that energy to flow by giving away whatever you have accumulated and don't need anymore.

- Circulate positive ideas. Give to your environment your best thoughts and feelings.

- Stop consuming excessively. What you have too much of in your life today may become a lack in the future.

- Take good care of your health. To be a good provider, you also need to give yourself a chance to be well and in tune with your life force.

Develop a Liberating Attitude

The ego can sometimes imprison you in beliefs and values of the past that are no longer worthy of your attention. You act in a liberating way when you breathe in deeply the light of the Soul. In the presence of that loving light your inner potential for renewal is revealed and limiting beliefs are dissolved. To live entirely in the present moment is the most liberating attitude there is.

Practical Suggestions for a Liberating Attitude

- Start to do today what you said you would do yesterday.

- Release that last little thread of mistrust that holds you from relaxing completely.

- Liberate the tenseness on your forehead, worrying less, and giving more attention to the wonders of each present moment.

- Observe a bird in flight. Fly away with it.

Develop a Paternal Attitude

Anyone who acts in a paternal way will radiate a lot of energy and vitality. Love will be present in the effort to know what is yet unknown, and love will be motivating the action to create what has been envisioned. The archetypal energy of the "father" within inspires enthusiasm and shows the way to use willpower with love. This is an attitude that stimulates and gives birth to creativity.

Practical Suggestions for a Paternal Attitude

- Without doubting follow your intuitive hunch.

- Dare to say to someone, in an elegant and loving way, that which you were afraid to say.

- Be a living example of the kind of leader who follows the guidance and wisdom of the heart.

- Keep your vision clear, your spine erect, and your heart in peace.

Develop a Compassionate Attitude

The compassionate attitude unites you through Love with all the sentient beings in the Universe of God. You are acting compassionately when you can feel in your heart the same way the other is feeling with no sense of separation. It is the Love of the Soul that inspires compassion and creates an inner space in consciousness where the other can be received, exactly as he or she or it is, in the eternal present.

Practical Suggestions for a Compassionate Attitude

- Accept and love yourself as you are, unconditionally.

- Practice the presence of the Soul in your life. Feel the Soul as if it were your beloved partner or your deeply loved child.

- Don't be in a hurry. The ship won't leave the shore until everyone is on it.

- Have you watered your plants today? Have you held someone today? Have you cared for your loving pet?

Develop a Pragmatic Attitude

*I*f you want to live significant experiences, you need to have an open mind and two feet on the ground. Thinking too much—or idly dreaming—can hinder the evolution of a process that is already clear. Truth can only be understood when you put it into practice. When you act in a pragmatic way, you are going to be totally practical and will always find the way to transform an ideal into reality.

Practical Suggestions for a Pragmatic Attitude

- Observe your use of words. It is important to practice what you preach.

- Make that dream come true. If it's building a house, start by buying a lock for the door; take the first step, even if the walk will take a thousand steps.

- Get in touch with the practical and sensible side of your feminine inner polarity.

- Find the most practical and simple way to get to your goal. Avoid unnecessary complications.

Develop a Poetic Attitude

*T*o develop a poetic attitude you need to be aware of the beauty, the rhythm, and the most creative expression that you can manifest in moments of inspiration. The muse within you will come out and joyfully express herself whenever you notice the greatness of life. She will synthesize it in clear and simple language that springs from the heart. The power of a poetic attitude lies in the gentle expression of beauty, which brings meaning to every little detail, and rhymes with the joy you want to express.

Practical Suggestions for a Poetic Attitude

- Use your creative imagination more. Add meaningful details to your environment by cultivating beauty with simplicity.

- Notice the flowers and the birds in your city. Smell their fragrance—listen to their song.

- In life, in traffic, in line while you wait, kiss the joy as it flies!

- "To be great, be whole; do not exclude or exaggerate what is yours" (Fernando Pessoa).

Develop a Modest Attitude

When you develop a modest attitude you will attract favorable situations. This is so because you are aware of the value of being humble. True humbleness can be grasped when you perceive that all that has been filled will eventually be emptied, and all that ascends will descend some day. Exercising this attitude develops a sense of equality, helps in the simplification of strategies, and doesn't superimpose conditions. Behind the modest attitude lies the true greatness of a person.

Practical Suggestions for a Modest Attitude

- Do your job without calling attention to yourself. Recognize that doing things with loving care gives you a lot of satisfaction.

- Do something you think is important, but be free from glamour.

- Be a charming person, naturally. Have faith in your singularity and uniqueness.

- Modesty and persistence go well together. The modesty of water is capable of wearing away rock.

Develop an Innocent Attitude

*I*t is only possible to develop an innocent attitude when you feel free from guilt. When a child is learning to walk and falls, the child innocently gets up and tries again. If the child felt guilty about the fall, he or she would have a lot of trouble trying to walk again. The innocent attitude is not aiming at profits and has no hidden agendas; the child only responds to the present moment with spontaneous simplicity. Innocence is connected with the Soul, and because it fosters uncomplicated behavior, it is easy and natural to move ahead.

Practical Suggestions for an Innocent Attitude

- Notice if you are expressing tenderness and care for yourself. This opens doors for you to do the same with others.

- Be inspired by young children by watching them in action. Try to reconnect with your inner child.

- The only antidote for guilt is forgiveness. Surrender to the Love of the Soul and forgive yourself.

- Live the present moment with the enthusiasm of a child.

Develop a Telepathic Attitude

*T*he telepathic attitude will take you into dimensions of true communication. If you have synchronized with this attitude today, you will certainly become aware of the importance of knowing how to listen. True communication happens when you know how to listen to the voice of the Soul in the silence of your consciousness. So it is probable that the invitation today is to be more in the listening mode than in the talking one. If you proceed in this way, you may have a chance to channel the right words at the right moment.

Practical Suggestions for a Telepathic Attitude

- Follow the telepathic impulses that come into your mind. Pay attention to the thoughts and images that come through with the luminous quality of a clear understanding. Radiate them.

- Visualize creative and positive images reflected in areas of planet Earth that may need healing and spiritual awakening.

- Lend your ears to your heart. In listening to it, you learn the art of expressing the best of yourself.

- Use well the gift of telecommunications. Notice if you are keeping your telephone conversations in a pattern of time and quality you have consciously chosen.

Develop a *Harmonious Attitude*

*I*n Nature everything is interrelated and works interdependently. If your lifestyle is dull or you don't feel you have any meaningful interactions, maybe you have forgotten, momentarily, that you are part of a great system of harmonious relationships. So, you need to emphasize the strength of your relationships and not the hierarchical position you occupy at home or at work. Developing a harmonious attitude will show you the best way to express the human values you want to put into action. You are a living system of relationships and meaningful experiences, and all parts are fundamentally important for the Whole.

Practical Suggestions for a Harmonious Attitude

- Believe in the power of teamwork. Get the team together at home to do housecleaning, mow the lawn, clean the garage, etc.

- Visualize yourself working with a team.

- Use products made by companies that subscribe to ecological ethics.

- Use ecology at home—clean up your mess without expecting someone to do it for you.

- Avoid the obsession of becoming a specialist in something. But be especially competent in everything you do.

Develop an Intuitive Attitude

Quiet yourself and listen to what your intuition may be willing to tell you. When the light of intuition is on, it will break through barriers of limiting logic or constraining thoughts, and lead you immediately to take "right action." Intuition leaves no doubt behind. This is an attitude that you need to practice with clear intention because, as you allow reason to be included in the light of intuition, you will know directly what you really need to know. With the awakening of the Soul in your heart, the intuitive faculty will emerge as a natural gift and a talent that will light your way.

Practical Suggestions for an Intuitive Attitude

- Pay attention to the intuitive sensations that may come through your body.

- Be in harmony with your subconscious mind—feeling and thinking positively. It guards and opens your intuitive channel with the Soul.

- Discover ways to nourish the right hemisphere of your brain. Do things with your nondominant hand and exercise your creativity.

- Avoid long hours of intellectual exercise that may stress your mind. Create a silent space in the mind and learn to incubate your questions.

- Be joyful and creative; get out of your routine for a change.

Develop an Enthusiastic Attitude

When the fire of enthusiasm is lit in your consciousness you begin to have a genuine interest in all you want to accomplish. The ardor of wanting to do and give the best of yourself is united with the lightness and freedom of joy. Then you know how to persist, even when challenges come on your way. An enthusiastic attitude energizes you with a creative and divine fire, and the energy is always there to give support. The result is a perfect surrendering to your Divine Essence.

Practical Suggestions for an Enthusiastic Attitude

- If you begin to love what you do, you will naturally be led to do what you love the most.

- Live in the company of your highest aspirations. Read books that stimulate your self-realization.

- Look for the best in people and situations. In the best of each person is the power to transform that which is not so good.

- Do your work with passion and ardor.

Develop an Organized Attitude

There are many ways to put your life in order, and an organized attitude will let you perceive the unique order of every person, event, or circumstance. Things flow better and more naturally when you organize your life according to principles of flexibility, recognizing priorities and the wise use of time. When you develop an organized attitude, you will see the rhythm and the ritual in everything you do. You'll understand your integrity and your interdependence with the environment in which you live.

Practical Suggestions for an Organized Attitude

- Make good use of your time. Be aware of the priorities of each moment of your life.

- Plan the activities on your agenda. Try to follow your plan. Order and flexibility can make a good blend.

- Notice your daily rituals. Perceive the quality of attention you have been giving them. For example, tune in to taking a shower, brushing your teeth, driving your car, or enjoying your meals.

- Discover different ways of organizing things. Look at people and situations from a sense of inner order that is unique for everyone.

Develop a Tolerant Attitude

*A*n inner power comes to your rescue if you choose to develop a tolerant attitude when faced with challenges. These challenges are instrumental in encouraging growth. You can see that it's necessary to endure a little more, without creating opposition or antagonism to some current situation. When a tolerant attitude develops it's because you have decided to support something a little longer. You know that this time will bring a higher perspective to your vision. To be tolerant is to be able to respond according to circumstances, without hurting or being hurt, because you are empowered by the loving presence of the Soul.

PRACTICAL SUGGESTIONS FOR A TOLERANT ATTITUDE

- Notice if you are allowing any crystallized perceptions or beliefs to keep people away from you.

- Allow yourself to forgive those who don't see life as you do.

- Be tolerant with teens and children. But do not mistake tolerance for permissiveness. The first can expand awareness; the latter will blunt a loving intelligence.

- Be clear whenever you communicate your perceptions so that you can avoid misunderstandings before it may be too late.

Develop a Tranquil Attitude

When you are free from the anxiety of quick results, and perceive the importance of being aware of the whole process that each situation involves, then you can be tranquil. Tranquillity emerges from your being anchored in the wisdom of the Soul and its gifts—conscious speech with no superfluous words, the certainty that the most violent storm will pass, as well as the silencing of doubts in a tranquil heart.

Practical Suggestions for a Tranquil Attitude

- Try handicrafts. Find a weaving course, or a clay workshop, or simply do something that will allow you to use your hands in silence.

- Practice feeling the presence of the Soul in the center of your heart. Feel the tranquillity that comes when you are in touch with your deeper Self.

- Be thankful for moments of silence and solitude that life offers you. Try to listen to the silence in the middle of the agitation of this busy world.

- Release any attachment to your "human doing." Concentrate more on your "human being" whenever you do something.

Develop a Sensitive Attitude

Sensitivity will put you in touch with the present moment. And so you become aware of other people's feelings and attitudes and perceive their implications and nuances. Sensitivity, when inspired by the Soul, will take you to a level of awareness so you can see what is relevant and meaningful for the present moment. Developing a sensitive attitude will enable you to pay attention to the eternal present and solve the conflicts between what takes you back into the past or sends you forward to the future. To be sensitive is to be aware of the delicate etheric web that connects all human beings.

Practical Suggestions for a Sensitive Attitude

- Quiet your mind and pay attention to the thoughts that come as a detached observer.

- Pay attention to your gestures, and to the tenderness and gentleness that you can manifest in your life.

- Relate more consciously with the sounds and colors in your environment. Make use of appropriate colors. Notice the tone of your voice.

- How do you deal with your temperament? What have you been doing with your emotionally charged thoughts? Have you been paying attention to your inner child?

Develop a Passionate Attitude

When you develop a passionate attitude you get in touch with your capacity to go through any experience of life with a deep and sincere commitment to express love. Loving devotion gives you the incentive to go ahead naturally. Fear is dissolved as you find it more important to extend your arms to others and embrace them, rather than staying centered in your own little self. When you act passionately a subtle fire is lit in your heart and it lights up the path to be followed. Enlivened by a vital energy, you are ready to follow the guidance of the Soul.

This attitude opens the way to the powerful experience of surrendering to love.

PRACTICAL SUGGESTIONS FOR A PASSIONATE ATTITUDE

- Do something with great enthusiasm that you have wanted to do for a long time.

- Find things to do that will put you in closer contact with people and Nature.

- Practice surrender, releasing your attachments, beginning with the smaller ones. All that you release consciously will come back later, in a new level of awareness.

- Don't be afraid of intimacy. A passionate attitude will attract people who can serve as mirrors in which your true image can be reflected.

Develop a Rational Attitude

There are moments when the clarity of an ordered and understanding mind is like a fresh breeze alleviating oppressive emotions. When you need to develop a rational attitude, you will consider the facts with calm precision. This will allow true understanding. Thoughts that have been emotionalized are like humidity infiltrating and corroding your best intentions. A good dose of rationality is always welcome when there is an excess of emotionalism in the air.

Practical Suggestions for a Rational Attitude

- Set clear boundaries. They enable you to create intelligent interactions.

- Find ways of creating more order and discipline in your life.

- Organize your financial life. Keep your expenses within your budget, having always in mind what you earn and what you spend.

- Read a good book about how you can clarify your thinking and develop your creative imagination.

Develop a Patient Attitude

The patient attitude emerges spontaneously when you pay attention to the energy flow of each present moment. To develop this attitude it is necessary to stop hurrying and to avoid the impetus of emotion. In its place you can invoke a calm and wonderful capacity—that comes from the Soul—with inner security and strength you can withstand any challenges and changes to your plans. This attitude will give you a different way of dealing with clock time and you'll learn to flow with events as they unfold. What would happen if maternal patience were not there to support growth and development in Nature? Patience that comes from the Soul is an infinite source of safe support.

Practical Suggestions for a Patient Attitude

- Listen and try to better understand the different ways children express themselves whenever you are in touch with them.

- Be aware of an Angelic presence creating miracles whenever you see the best in people and situations.

- Slow the pace of your life by paying attention to the level of patience you manifest.

- Participate in group activities. Listen to people—allowing each one to have his or her turn.

Develop a Synergistic Attitude

The whole is always greater than the sum of its parts. When you develop a synergistic attitude, your attention is turned to the quality of what you can accomplish as a team. This attitude shows the real value of working in a group, allowing the energy to flow through everyone without concern for external authority or hierarchy. If you act with synergy in mind, you can accomplish much more, in less time, and achieve the best quality. When you develop a synergistic attitude, you will be open to receive the inspiration that comes from the Soul to create group harmony and you can help change the world.

Practical Suggestions for a Synergistic Attitude

- Be a living example for children. Listen to them with true interest and allow them to participate, in whatever way they can, in activities at home so they can develop the spirit of service for others.

- Observe yourself for a day, in order to become aware of how others have felt stimulated by your cooperative presence.

- Get involved with some cause that speaks directly to your heart.

- Value the activities you can do on a team. When you work with a shared vision and a clear purpose, total quality is always the result.

Develop a Flexible Attitude

To be flexible without fear or guilt is to be like water that will occupy the spaces that are available in the present moment. Water is adaptable and flows, filling any open spaces. It follows the basic laws of life—penetrating, purifying, and nourishing. Flexibility will connect you with the principles of fluidity and invites you to perceive the need to let things flow, to let things change, without losing touch with your true Essence.

Practical Suggestions for a Flexible Attitude

- Be aware of the movement and rhythm of your life. Be a silent witness and dance with the rhythm of what happens. With flexibility you cocreate the needed changes.

- Be kind, be flexible. At the least resistance do not insist. Do as water does—go around the stone on your way.

- See if you are carrying invisible burdens. Release the tenseness in your shoulders or jaw. When things do not flow the way you expect, there may be something hidden asking to be noticed and valued.

- Invite flexibility into your beliefs. Something you believe today may not be the same ten years later.

Develop a Thankful Attitude

*I*f you expand your consciousness to a point of greater inclusiveness, you will be immediately aware of how much you have to be thankful for. Nature gives herself abundantly through the air you breathe, the water you drink, and the minerals and plants that offer themselves for your nourishment and well-being. You will also notice the network of significant people who work anonymously so you can have comfort and facilities in your daily living. The attitude of thankfulness will connect you with divine grace, and if you start the day with thanks, you will become aware of the infinite gifts around you.

Practical Suggestions for a Thankful Attitude

- How do you start your day? Remember to give thanks for the wonderful gift of being alive and for the experiences that enrich your life.

- If you use the buses in your city, remember to thank the driver for the wonderful service. Don't forget the telephone operators, waiters, street cleaners, garbage collectors, and the teams that work so you can have electricity, water, gas. Remember to say an encompassing and vibrant THANK YOU!

- Be connected with your heart center whenever you say "thank you."

- To feel really thankful, it's necessary to recognize that natural resources are to be shared by all and must be used well. Feel yourself as part of the creation of divine abundance.

Develop a Receptive Attitude

A receptive attitude will put you in direct contact with the qualities of your feminine inner polarity. Receptivity will allow you to listen more intently so you can nurture people and situations silently and effectively. It doesn't matter if you are involved in an objective or subjective situation, the receptive attitude will welcome and absorb what happens in perfect relaxation. When you need to act with receptivity you will be leading while following. In being receptive you create an inner space of total clarity into which your consciousness is expanded to reveal what you need to learn.

Practical Suggestions for a Receptive Attitude

- Enjoy the moments when you can be alone with yourself to reflect and to listen to your Soul.

- Observe your reactions to the unexpected. If you know how to be receptive, there will be time and space for an intelligent reflection and response.

- Try relaxation exercises to release physical tension.

- Review your day. Can you think of three occasions when you have been kind to someone?

Develop a Positive Attitude

A positive attitude is one that invites you to give up extremist positions. You are invited to reach a point of synthesis and transcendence from where you can see the dynamic balance of opposites. From that point you can see everything from a broader perspective and discover a creative solution—immediately. Mental barriers are dissolved, and misunderstandings are clarified when you are willing to see the best in yourself and in others.

Practical Suggestions for a Positive Attitude

- Pay attention to any act of extreme polarization. Realize that everything, positive or negative, has its origin in the same principle—the Principle of Unity.

- See if you are putting your faith in exterior things only. It is important to depend on your Inner Divinity, the point of transcendence within yourself.

- Use your creative imagination, a gift from the Soul, to create only that which you want to see manifested in your life.

- Keep your mind flexible in face of any situation. In flexibility lies a great power to express a positive attitude.

Develop a Transformative Attitude

The crystal clear power of transformation will free you from fear and insecurity whenever you choose to express the best in yourself. When this happens, your body and personality are transformed into receptors and transmitters of the light of the Soul. Making changes in yourself, being free of the bondage of the past, brings liberation.

Practical Suggestions for a Transformative Attitude

- With determination, look at the parts of your personality that you would like to change. Accept them and release them into the light of the Soul to be purified.

- Liberate your life from everything you consider superfluous. Release everything that blocks you from being who you really are.

- Always remember your eternal inner child, who knows the process of transformation, and is always available when needed.

- Clean your house or get rid of something you no longer need so you can allow yourself to clean out old thoughts as well, for this begins the transformation process.

Develop an Optimistic Attitude

An optimistic attitude has the power to dissipate the fog that blocks your inner vision. Then you can concentrate on the power of the light and warmth of your inner Sun. The more you affirm the presence of that light and warmth, the more you will be creating the proper reality for each moment. The true optimistic attitude is not opposed to challenges that need to be faced and lived through, but it can transform those challenges into creative impulses that attract the best situations. When your creative energy is directed to create optimum conditions for your life, you are developing an optimistic attitude.

Practical Suggestions for an Optimistic Attitude

- Contemplate the beautiful and the best in people—benefits are mutual.

- Pay attention to the effects of your thoughts and emotions on the situations of your life. Whenever you follow the way you are reacting, you will have time to change the course of the energy you are using, if needed.

- Self-acceptance makes possible great changes. Practice it and true optimism will be a partner on your path.

- Every correct action will clear eventual misunderstandings. Every conscious relationship is an abundant source of optimism.

Develop a Maternal Attitude

When you use your capacity to nourish, to support, to accept, and to serve others you are exercising the maternal attitude. The maternal attitude liberates your talents to manifest feelings of sharing, of partnership, of solidarity, and it helps dissolve blocks caused by the excessive use of domination. The maternal aspect within is going to unconditionally support every being, every thing or process that will need strength and nourishment to evolve and grow. This attitude creates space to receive your best expectations, and lovingly provides the means for the birth of everything into light.

Practical Suggestions for a Maternal Attitude

- The maternal within is naturally modest and free from compulsion. Let yourself be delighted in whatever you may be doing today.

- Try to feel the moments in which you surrender to the acts of giving and receiving. Then go beyond giving and receiving and concentrate on "surrender."

- See if you are aware of the difference between principle and process. The maternal attitude understands the principle, but surrenders to the process of seeing something coming to birth.

- Take good care of your home, your clothes, your belongings. Be a good guardian of Mother Earth's gifts to you.

Develop a Healing Attitude

Planet Earth has never been in such need of healing as in this present moment. Your healing attitude is needed so humans can begin to waken and transform everything that was done to Earth in the past through ignorance and carelessness. This healing will be processed with greater intensity when you recognize that, on the Soul level, you have all the healing potential you need. You can heal the planet and yourself when you are free from negativity and ignorance. Then you can choose to channel your creative potential to receive and radiate the Love that comes from the Soul.

Practical Suggestions for a Healing Attitude

- Practice forgiveness. Without forgiveness healing is not possible. It is as if you are chained to the person or situation that you need to forgive. Forgiveness liberates these chains.

- Practice the presence of the Soul. Create an inner Temple of Light in your meditation and transform it into a place of personal and planetary healing.

- Allow the Angels to participate in your life. Invoke their presence and let your life be filled with joy and light.

- Pay attention to what you "take in" physically, emotionally, and mentally.

Develop a Committed Attitude

When you make a true commitment, all the energy that comes from higher levels of your consciousness is available to bring the help you need. The attitude of commitment liberates you from the need to do things out of duty or obligation, because you start to trust in your potential completely. When you can create a committed attitude it's because you've reached a point of maturity where you know that, without vocation and self-giving, no project can evolve on the physical plane. When you are fully committed to your Inner Essence and to the

Spirit that permeates all life, then the Angels of God will be ready to help wherever they are needed.

Practical Suggestions for a Committed Attitude

- Decide to accept positions of leadership that are being offered. Follow the guidance of your Soul and be your own leader.

- Commit yourself to activities that give you joy. Be responsible for the presence of delight in your life.

- Commit yourself to finishing any unfinished "business." Establish a period of time and a final date to see the project concluded.

- What is the most important commitment of your life? If you know it clearly, your actions and decisions will be strengthened by this clarity.

Develop a Supportive Attitude

When the development of the ego is detrimental to the development and the awakening of the Soul in your heart, you will be facing a situation that will not sustain itself for very long. But when the emphasis is in the development of the personality in tune with the Soul, you will create a safe and healthy environment for the manifestation of Divinity in your life. A supportive attitude will lead you to think of more than the immediate results and profits from your actions. Above all, you will take action after you take into account what those actions will mean for all sentient beings who share the same environment, breathe the same air, and participate in the same biosphere.

Practical Suggestions for a Supportive Attitude

- Notice what you are doing today that will have very important consequences in the future.

- Accept the diversity of thought and culture where you live and work. The world is self-sustainable because it is rich in diversities that support each other in a perfect web of relationships.

- Recognize those attitudes in your life that are not supportive anymore. Replace them with others that are in tune with your values and the quality of your consciousness.

- Be aware of how you use planetary resources. Help world economy by not wasting food or drink; planning the use of your car daily; giving away clothes and things that you don't use anymore; using water, electricity, and fuel with consciousness.

Develop a Practical Attitude

When you are supported by common sense and recognize the need to act according to the basic principles of natural law, you are developing a practical attitude. In doing this, you know that it's very important to identify the universal principles that rule the processes of growth and evolution. You also will be able to admit that you have lessons to learn with each situation that happens in your life. Your ego can be very insensible, mainly when you lose the notion of limits and forget that human wakening is gradual. To use common sense is to know how to proceed, step by step, dealing with whatever comes with an open mind and in tune with the present moment.

PRACTICAL SUGGESTIONS FOR A PRACTICAL ATTITUDE

- Cultivate an inner strength and an outer serenity. In face of complicated situations, be patient and kind to yourself and to others.

- Search for truth openly, without rigidity, and the secrets of the Universe will be revealed to you.

- Recognize the wisdom of the most experienced. There are moments when common sense would allow you to ask for help from the wiser ones.

- Don't procrastinate after you recognize a mistake. It is better to recognize and clear it now than to have to face retribution later.

Develop a Sincere Attitude

A sincere attitude will put you in touch with your true feelings and thoughts in any situation. The liberation of hypocrisy and pretense will allow the mind and heart to be more constructive and happy. To reach the ideal solution to a challenging issue it is very important that you become receptive to truth and express it with the right words. The sincere attitude flows naturally when you are willing to liberate prejudices and dissolve limiting beliefs. Honesty and sincerity are synonyms in bringing the inner peace that flows naturally when you are in tune with your Soul.

Practical Suggestions for a Sincere Attitude

- Become aware of the things that trigger your negative reactions. These triggers are a revealing source of shadowy aspects that you don't like to accept as being part of yourself.

- Sincerity doesn't mean that everything should be said, no matter what. Genuine sincerity reveals the truth about yourself and others at the right time, and in the right place, in a loving and respectful way.

- Find ways of improving your verbal expression. Speak words that stimulate and reveal the essence of every creature in this world.

- Every time you look at yourself in the mirror, feel a sincere appreciation for yourself. Feel the inner power that comes when you are sincere.

Develop a Harmless Attitude

*T*o develop a harmless attitude you need to be open to the higher levels of your consciousness. Harmlessness is one of the most needed attitudes on Earth these days. When you recognize the creative power that you have in your thoughts and words, you can begin to abstain from actions and words that may harm others. Life flows freely and abundantly when your being is in harmony, and words and gestures are used to create a caring world.

Practical Suggestions for a Harmless Attitude

- Choose a day in the week to pay total attention to your words. Try to speak only those words that are necessary.

- Smile more. Relax the muscles of your face intentionally.

- Cultivate constructive and positive thoughts. In this way you practice harmlessness for yourself and the world.

- At least once a week, remember to thank all the creatures in nature that are participating in the creation of your nourishment.

Develop a Connected Attitude

Like the air we breathe, a connected attitude brings vitality and reveals your interdependence with the living world around you. When you are connected, your attention is always turned to what is relevant in the present. You don't waste energy with unnecessary distractions. The connection with the essential quality of each person or being of Nature creates a vibrant and meaningful link allowing communication to happen without effort. Connecting with your Soul in the silence of the heart opens the way to the transforming power of clear intuition.

Practical Suggestions for a Connected Attitude

- Do regular exercises to train your attention. Start by organizing your life better, and taking care of the smallest details.

- Develop a conscious partnership with your subconscious mind, nourishing it with positive thoughts and words.

- Learn from your mistakes. This can strengthen your connection with the Soul and develop the quality of your attention.

- Calm your emotions by developing the habit of "walking them away." When your emotions control you, they block the way to your connection with your Soul.

Develop an Intelligent Attitude

This is the moment to invoke the genius you carry within. The intelligent attitude will let you know what is the best for all in a certain situation; it will show the meaning behind the learning process that is taking place. To act with intelligence is to be able to respond with full loving attention to what life is proposing. It also indicates the ability to see that challenges are a living sign that something in you is out of alignment with the cosmic order. To know how to read these signs in the living "Book of Nature," is the most efficient exercise to reveal the brilliance of intelligence within your Soul.

Practical Suggestions for an Intelligent Attitude

- Recognize the source of inner power that comes from your Soul. Security and happiness are rooted within yourself.

- Take care not to become "the owner of truth." Just be a living example of what is truthful for you.

- Recognizing limitations on the physical plane is an act of intelligence. Transcending them with the help of the light and love of the Soul is genius.

- Follow your inner truth, and whoever is on the same vibration will be attracted to you and you can create together. Real intelligence is selfless.

Develop a Detached Attitude

The more connected you are with the Soul, the more free you will be from the need of possessing things, people, and situations. When your actions are motivated by love, an attitude of detachment will permeate your Being. You can choose to participate in the events of life free from mental negativity, or outbursts of emotional reactions. With an attitude of detachment your senses will be at peace and you will understand the deep meaning of impermanence. Everything is changing continuously and life is always abundant when you are detached from the results of your action.

Practical Suggestions for a Detached Attitude

- Discover ways of helping others, but without playing the "savior." Liberate everyone in God's care, after you have given the best of yourself.

- Find ways of serving in the city where you live. Start by releasing any paranoid beliefs and act with simplicity.

- Release the need to rush ahead when moments of adversity arise. Pause for reflection and try to discern the teaching that is coming from your Soul in this experience.

- Sometimes it is necessary to release an attitude, a relationship, or even a goal, to allow the higher energy of the Soul to guide you toward the right path. When you accept this situation with detachment, it always brings the best for all.

Develop a
Dynamic Attitude

A dynamic attitude is like an inner fire that lights up and drives you to act with readiness and vitality. When you develop a dynamic attitude, you make things happen, and effectively create clear communication between people and what is to be done. Inertia has no place in your life. True dynamism emerges like a beam of purifying light that transforms doubts and feelings of inability into the certainty that you can move ahead safely. Changes are processed in a natural way, according to universal law, and all you have to do is to respond the Soul guidance with readiness.

Practical Suggestions for a Dynamic Attitude

- Make a list of the things you want to accomplish this week/month/year; place this list in a visible place and plan how you will accomplish your goals.

- Practice sports or take morning walks in Nature. Keep your body fit.

- What do you like fixing? What improvements can you make now in your home, in your car, at work?

- Find something to celebrate every day. Recognize the great gift of being alive and aware of God's presence in your heart.

Develop a Healthy Attitude

Deep within your heart you carry the memory of a perfect and vital state of health. To develop a healthy attitude requires remembering that you are permeated by an inner electromagnetic power that vivifies you with Divine Love and Light. The state of total health is manifested when you choose to respond lovingly and carefully to the needs of your body, emotions, and mind, and be in tune with the will of your Soul. When you do this for yourself, you also learn to do it for Earth, where you live, which is the only source of physical nourishment for your existence.

Practical Suggestions for a Healthy Attitude

- Develop new nourishing habits. Ask within what is the best nutrition for you and follow the guidance.

- What do you do that adds value to your health and to the environment around you?

- See if you are "talking" more about your health than "doing something" to keep it in good condition.

- Develop a capacity for creating limits and being able to say "no" to people and situations that do not promote your health.

Index

adaptable, 24
alternative, 22
altruistic, 58
appreciative, 34
bold, 8
committed, 116
compassionate, 66
connected, 126
consistent, 42
cooperative, 14
decisive, 12
detached, 130
diplomatic, 26
dynamic, 132
efficient, 10
enthusiastic, 82
flexible, 100
focused, 48
generous, 18
giving, 60
harmless, 124
harmonious, 78

healing, 114
healthy, 134
impeccable, 44
innocent, 74
intelligent, 128
intuitive, 80
joyful, 40
liberating, 62
loving, 16
maternal, 112
mature, 56
meditative, 50
modest, 72
optimistic, 110
organized, 84
participatory, 28
passionate, 92
paternal, 64
patient, 96
persevering, 52
pleasurable, 46
poetic, 70

positive, 106
practical, 120
pragmatic, 68
pure, 36
rational, 94
receptive, 104
responsible, 32
reverent, 54
sensitive, 90
sensual, 38
sincere, 122
supportive, 118
synergistic, 98
telepathic, 76
thankful, 102
tolerant, 86
tranquil, 88
transformative, 108
truthful, 30
wise, 20

About the Author

Sônia Café was born in Salvador, Brazil, and spent many years studying and actually living within a spiritual community. Theosophy, Alice Bailey, Ken Carey, Rudolf Steiner, Geoffrey Hodson, the mystics, the Findhorn Community—are all sources of inspiration for her. Café is the author of the best-selling *Meditating with the Angels*, and *Transforming Dragons*, both published by Weiser. She lives in São Paulo, and is affiliated with Editora Pensamento, a major publishing house in Brazil.

About the Illustrator

Neide Innecco has been painting professionally since 1968. She has illustrated a number of children's books, and is known for her angel paintings. She is the artist for *Meditating with the Angels*, which was written by Sônia Café (Weiser, 1994). In addition to painting, Innecco has been interested in spiritual studies, spending time in India and founding the Shanti Academy of Yoga and the Center for Spiritual Studies, both in Brazil. She lives in São Paulo, Brazil, and has five children and nine grandchildren.